Minimize Considered

poems by

Nina Murray

Finishing Line Press
Georgetown, Kentucky

Minimize Considered

Copyright © 2018 by Nina Murray
ISBN 978-1-63534-509-4 First Edition
All rights reserved under International and Pan-American Copyright Conventions. No part of this book may be reproduced in any manner whatsoever without written permission from the publisher, except in the case of brief quotations embodied in critical articles and reviews.

ACKNOWLEDGMENTS

Several poems in this collection have been previously published as follows:

In English and Lithuanian translation in the anthology of the 2012 Druskininkai Poetic Fall festival: "let us speak of a stone."
"December," under the title "December 14," and "Acquired Tastes" in *Cosmonauts' Avenue*, 1.7
"The Discreet Charm of the Bourgeoisie" in *Canthius* I, 2015.
"All Enemies, Foreign and Domestic" in *Lumina*, Vol. XVI
"June" in *Xanadu* 2018

Publisher: Leah Maines
Editor: Christen Kincaid
Cover Art and Design: Nina Murray
Author Photo: Nina Murray

Printed in the USA on acid-free paper.
Order online: www.finishinglinepress.com
also available on amazon.com

Author inquiries and mail orders:
Finishing Line Press
P. O. Box 1626
Georgetown, Kentucky 40324
U. S. A.

Table of Contents

August 1

October 2

December 3

Departures 4

Secure Documents 6

The Hegemonist 8

the chinese were wrong 9

November 10

December 12

The Discreet Charm of the Bourgeoisie 13

Customs and Border Protection Case Notes, expanded ... 15

Four Lunches in Downtown Toronto 16

Acquired Tastes 17

The Fates 18

Four Changes of Station 19

Minimize Considered 25

June 26

June, Hoary Plantain 27

All Enemies, Foreign and Domestic 28

Cooking Dinner on the Night before Moving 30

U.S. Department of State Foreign Affairs Manual Volume 5

Handbook 1 Correspondence Handbook:

...non-urgent, nonessential message traffic must be curtailed or reduced to a post that does not possess the means to process a normal telegraphic workload. All cable traffic... must contain the phrase "Minimize Considered" as the last item of text, prior to the signature

August

The spiders are comfortable here
on the east face of the building
in the lambent glow of CBC's riddled logo next door

anchored in the joint of brushed steel
the height doesn't bother them
the wind
seventeen floors above the street
fawns over them
feeds small flies into their web
an occasional disoriented wasp
it is a life

the other day I saw a hawk
alight on the cornice of an office tower
so distant that if I hadn't caught the instant
of his wings folding
feet outstretched in anticipation of landing
I would've mistaken his small
chiseled shape for an accoutrement
a concrete outgrowth
a stalagmite

so do we inhabit
this city's crevices
its aeries
crags
rooftops
and wedge ourselves in
a toehold
a storefront
adapt quickly
invent identities
paint signs
The Barking Squirrel
Raven's Knickers
Blooming Fools

October

The chestnuts are accommodating creatures,
ready to turn their latticework canopies an early, luminous gold,
transport me with the scent, the breath of cracked shells underfoot.
The transposition of place sudden and undeniable; my soul reduced
to an iteration of a certain latitude, suddenly at home half-way
around the world.
They must not be allowed to grow as large as in the old country,
for fear of weak limbs, treacherous, crumbling trunks,
disease incompatible with the responsible management
of this urban environment, but they are here nonetheless, generous
in their ministrations to the light, serene
in their gentle, gracious shedding of leaves, each curved slice of yellow
gliding downward without haste—giving the spectator time to conceive a
    metaphor,
the leaf as the curving brush on the surface of air—
and the deposit of chestnuts themselves on the lawn, all of them
cracked and nibbled and then abandoned by squirrels.
I looked for an unsullied one, but couldn't find any—
if I had, I would have put one in my pocket and carried it around,
perfectly smooth and silky, irresistible in the purposefulness of its density
and weight, a most perfect lambent thing that begins fading
the moment it seduces you to make it yours.

December

This week, I've been dealing with mine engineers a lot,
and found myself looking at them as one does at a certain kind
of dog one imagines adopting—I wonder what it would be like
to have one of my own, a clear-eyed millwright, say,
or a die-cutter. This air of habitual accomplishment, of having the uncertainties
of the world resolved daily into tension ratios, loads, forces
applied and resisted, their routine unraveling of the cosmos
into small, manageable tasks—I wonder what it would be like to have
that around, and the way I look at them, one by one, as they tell me
they've been with the company seven years, eight, twelve—it treats its
people right, ma'am—
must be doing something to make them rib each other, laugh at
the small joke I make about someone ending up the superintendent
of buckets, which is true, it's what you do when you dedicate yourself
to things like rope tensioners, hoists, and shaft-sinking plants,
mine-building being an enterprise of tremendous commitment
and, surely, liability, but also, I sense, one that preserves boyhood,
arrests it, in fact, traps the tinkering we've all outgrown
and nurtures it in distant, protected realms of industrial serenity—
places with names like North Bay, Uma, or Elco,
and when they leave, my exotic, rare species, I miss them a little,
and keep thinking of them boarding small planes in their chinos, certainly,
carrying backpacks—a voyeur by accident, I'm loath to stop.

Departures

I
Boarding a train such a different undertaking
from flying—still free from the technocratic
teleology of gates and chutes,
the platform—mythically two-faced—
tantalizing in its promise of error
of the possibility to choose the wrong side,
board the wrong train,
turn one's back on oneself and depart
in the opposite direction.

II
I recognize this:
the way she has the cash neatly pressed in her wallet,
the way she releases two immaculate bills to hand him
for some anticipated transaction,
and the way he has to turn them, have them face the same way,
before he puts them into his pocket. They negotiate
coats and canes, he in the aisle seat, she at the window,
they bump into each other's extremities, object-to-face,
elbow-to-armpit, unapologetic
as a pair of pebbles rubbed together
by tides.
I don't have to look. I know you are watching them too.
I know what you are thinking.

III
The cats I feed for you in your empty apartment
are not bothered by having been left behind.
They shed, contemplate the view, sit in the corners,
sense, perhaps, an occasional urgency to be elsewhere soon
—but this is relieved by finding the litter-box. Cats carry on
using your space, watch your ghost cross
the room, keep the shapes alert in their jobs
of accommodating—them, you. I think the cats know
their ontological role: they hold down the fort,
and aren't fooled, oh not at all, when it's me
they find at the door.

Secure Documents
> *National identity documents are printed utilizing a number of specialized techniques, such as intaglio, watermarking, or optically variable color-changing inks to prevent forgery.*

I
It is important, I was told, to spot the exploding maple leaves,
but I kept looking at the three silhouettes
of the geese, iconic in turquoise and periwinkle,
gazing eastward.

II
Ribbons in the mane of the lion,
mottos in Latin, reflected in the eagle's eye,
hidden maps, invisible seals—
the art matters. Engravers
spend years apprenticed to the Swiss,
learning, no doubt, among other things,
the proper pronunciation of words like
guilloche and *cloisonné.*
Forgery is the last bastion of taste;
the philistines who let their aesthetic
standards flag go to jail.
I sense
an opportunity for the other arts:
let me pen haiku by hand
on hundred dollar bills. Let
the novelist contribute a story
to the American passport. We do so yearn
to be in wide circulation,
watermarked into bond paper,
etched into polycarbon.

III
Some distant day,
someone will disinter, rather by accident,
our very durable passports
and leafing through them,
as I do every day,
perhaps think us disproportionately virtuous
for outfitting each citizen
with a pocket necropolis
of toucans, lemurs, prairies
and magnificent steel bridges,
all intricately preserved in true, brilliant
colors to serve as an aid in personal penance,
a gazetteer of sins.

The Hegemonist

> *The Hegemonist was a blog, run by a U.S. Diplomat and occasionally critical of the State Department's actions. It ceased publication suddenly and without explanation a few years ago.*

The hegemonist was last seen
on the bank of a river
insisting
that politics end at the water's edge.
It is common to imagine him
driven there by a hostile force,
but in fact he was merely
a sensible young man in a charcoal suit
who had just disembarked
and could sense, behind him,
the juggernaut that delivered him there
rapidly sinking.

the chinese were wrong

with their octagonal charts of feng-shui
the elements mixed in a neat circle
lined up
the fifth substance is not
wood
but mud
the suction of this land on my soles
the homunculus brew of leaves
left where they've fallen
and a million steps
crushing piercing tattooing
our presence
        mine
                yours
                        ghosts
mud kissing itself whole
over and over

November

there must be poets in here somewhere
outnumbering the rectangular cells of high-rises
a hundred to one
a swarming film of humanity
inside the tessellated glass
but all I can see is shafted veins
pumping elevators

the myths we've learned to love
do not abide
all archetypes a century newer:
the grocer's Punjabi, the barber's Iranian,
and just as we speak the actuarial accountants from Shanghai
are taking a crack at an object's likelihood to be
in two places at once because
quantum physics employs
risk assessment
as much as hedge-funds do

you ask what my world is like and I say
beauty thwarted

one learns to live as a scavenger
hunt for bits of coherence
because that's how this city produces—
a box perhaps
set on a sidewalk
and labeled books
but containing instead
two very clean glass bottles
cushioned in an indigo terrycloth rag
a bright yellow muffin tin
the entire set
perfect as a Vermeer

let us speak of a stone
on a hushed winter beach far north
where we had once walked
the event
growing irrelevant every day
the rock
fingered by wave
after wave
holds sand in its pores
each grain nestled precisely
as in a dream of a honeycomb

how it must hum
with its illusion of swimming
when the thrusting water rolls
slides above it
retreats
pulls sand from around its waist
bares the roots beneath
the sensation of lift
unmistakably real

each rock alone
senses motion
its knowledge of freedom unseen
unknown
to the other stones
from that distant beach—
the ones we picked
and carried home

December

you cough every few steps
the sound and strain pointless
vain
self-reinforcing
something inside you
seemingly gone beyond the remedy
of the gently chilling air
and the good cheer of blue icicle lights
goat cheese
cobblestones
the whole riotous indulgence
of Montreal at Advent
    pink-camouflage-trousered cops
    handcuff elf-hatted pick-pockets
you tell me you still want
to be the man ahead of us on the sidewalk
out for a stroll with his wife
smoking a cigar
    down by the Vieux Port
    the carriage horses end their shift
    and we stop to let them pass
    two dusty
    muscled
    gray Percherons
    they break into a trot
    going home
    strike sparks from the stones
you tell me certain pleasures
are not vouchsafed to us

The Discreet Charm of the Bourgeoisie

I
a late-morning snowfall
watched from the seventeenth-floor window
free and convivial
sanguine in its proximity to the low
pearlescent clouds
joyful with the anticipation of settling
on the outstretched arms of the trees below
small perfect perches

II
a bottle of wine picked up on the way home from work
leather gloves
a modest aspiration to delight a friend with a Christmas gift
and you
quoting Kissinger over dinner

III
a girl would cross an ocean
for the promise of a man she could expect to civilize
that's how Quebec got started
four hundred years ago—
with a paid passage and a dowry
for able-bodied Normandiennes
who'd answer the call from their King

I may be a belated *Fille du Roi* (the dowries
were being paid in livestock long before my time)
but this is why I came—to bring you names
for your old-fashioned heart's desires:
civility
discernment
privacy
the discreet charm of the bourgeoisie

the age of moral heroism is always past
the deeds are done by others
and the consequences bequeathed to others still

IV
the leave to imagine myself
painting in oils en plein air
a keeper of a shop
the inventory neatly split
between arts home goods antiques
riding a mule down a snow-bound lane
I can almost feel the animal's shoulders
glide under the warm skin
tectonic   solid
I am good at this—seeing myself
traverse the world by means that are more dignified
or sometimes just different from what's available
toward ends unclear
as in my dreams I am unconcerned by
direction or accomplishment of a chore
but merely enamored of the clean swing of an axe in my grip
as it accelerates into the piece of wood
to be made fire
what's not to love about this lady farmer bodhisattva of mine—
it is perfectly unattainable and therefore
endlessly sustaining

Customs and Border Protection Case Notes, expanded

The Subjects were encountered after they'd crossed the bridge
on one of those days when the wind penetrates
the suspension cables and rages inside their vascular coils
like a trapped sentient virus. They stated they were traveling,
the two of them, to New Jersey, to attend the funeral of a man
they could not name and did not appear to know,
but someone had called, they said,
and asked them to come. They carried
a check for six thousand dollars, the name also left blank—
they said they were to give it to someone at the funeral. We felt
the bridge shuddering under our feet,
regular, percussive spasms in the concrete,
in our bones. The canine refused
to interact with the Subjects, instead giving us a look
some were inclined to interpret as pitying—we've reason to suspect
he knows more than any of us. The Subjects waited.
Their names meant nothing to our acronymed databases. Below the bridge,
and the pall of water that spawns the winds here,
we remembered the ships, frozen and barnacled on the rocks,
invisible and forgotten—struck en route to neither one of these shores.
The Subjects, wearing scarves, asked or added nothing.
Our own insistence on purpose of travel, ties, intent
did not seem to apply; this bridge,
this river—we found ourselves wondering, for an instant,
who conceived of putting us here, appointed us
toll masters on the edge of what we know, demanding explanations?
The fog came down, the noise of the wind in the cables the only proof
of the bridge's existence. The Subjects said they intended
to return, but wouldn't be going back the way they came.
If they had come to fetch a soul in need of passage to the other side
of oblivion, what would they say to us other than what they had already
    said?

Slow as a galley, their black Oldsmobile eased out into the fog.

Four Lunches in Downtown Toronto

I
dwell
under the layered entrapment of light
in the crab-apple blossoms
each petal a pink simmering ladle

II
observe
two men at the studious work
of training the stubby snouts of the municipal fountain
to spit just so
above the wading pool
their ladder a spindly siege tower
aimed at nothing

III
consider Churchill
the painter in his later years
see the harvest of ash drop from the cigar
into his palette
see him insouciantly work it into the ochres

IV
negotiate with the sparrow
until he won't take the flake of bread that's too big
a thing whose abundance puts it beyond
the category of need
he eyes it
then leaves

Acquired tastes

…and none of them useful or meritorious
a much-scraped palimpsest of things—lives, maybe—
that had already been
whence, I suppose, this affinity for my old, brindled dog,
a direct descendant of those stone-age
canids who fed on trash heaps
before people figured they could keep the dogs
if they didn't throw trash on a heap
so far from the cave
and the making of lists
which so compels me to make every poem a catalogue
of something if it's only my own
shortcomings
especially then
indeed—martinis
may be one worth listing
and the way one feels with a martini glass
watching the slow, pearlescent
crawl of vermouth around the rim
the olive perceptive
like the eye of the dog
attuned
to the imminent failure of fingers
grasping the food
and a scrap
falling
again

The Fates

> ...ghosts hide in the steel like heavy-armed men in mirrors
> Carl Sandburg

I found three women at the Wycliffe Barns
one had put out lemon tarts
the other—brownies
and the third one
demure snippets of green grapes
I took one and watched them work
on three parallel tables
the first hammered together
rectangles of wood and primed canvas
the second ran her bristle brushes
over the surface as we spoke
cadmium and smalt
converging in the vertigo of looking up
at the sky through the scrim of birch wood
the third woman sealed the work
with something that involved epoxy
she handled a blowtorch
smoothed the edges
with a spew of fire supple as her fingers
they wanted me to take something of theirs
home
but I kept thinking of the ghost of the hog
who'd given his bristles and the elderberry
crushed into paint and the punctured skin of crab-apples
oozing vermillion
and saw the hog laughing rolling
in the berries far under the epoxy's mirror
and wanted to leave him be
hidden beneath that scrim of leaves in the October sky

Four changes of station

1987, Sioux Falls, SD

I
When he thinks of the swimming pool
it is always summer, each day a protracted negotiation
between sunscreen, water, and light which fills the concrete
aperture of the pool tightly
like a heavy, well-fitted stamp.

The pool is in a municipal park,
an aspiring arcadia undercut by the commitment to efficiency
that is the ruling ethos of the place. The trees
are planted where they wouldn't drop leaves into the water.
The squirrels lope in haphazard zigzags between the trunks,
obviously lost. There is no shade.

The pool is open until dark. He watches
the vending machines, the dark semicircles in from of each,
the paths of wet footprints converging, constantly renewed
by the younger children, as if they didn't want to lose
critical evidence of their boredom and inflated desire to evaporation.

A girl, tan legs, hair in a wet ponytail,
on a chez lounge, with a book,
with a coke. The string of her tracks eroding,
but each time he looks he thinks the footprints are as narrow
as her soles.
When the dry concrete is no longer white, it is dusk.

Soon he can climb down. He hopes she will be one of the last
people to leave, so that he can affect a need to put away her chair,
strike up a conversation, maybe walk with her
to the parking lot. If she has a younger brother, they can linger
at the flood culvert where, he knows,
he can show the boy a turtle.

1997, Lincoln, NE

II
He likes to run on the winding sidewalks of subdivisions,
past the white-window-framed, single-garage ranch homes,
late-sixties atomic age angst gone to seed—
entire neighborhoods built not to be missed by the nuclear blast—
but each fold-on-itself house equipped with a basement
because certain death doesn't sell.

That's what his friend told him, the one who lives here—
she is at the curb this morning, salutes him with the trowel
which she'd been using to force apart clumps of iris bulbs.
He cannot tell if she's any good at her gardening.

Earlier, she would have read The Argus and The Star
to keep up with the obituaries and the petty misdeeds.
At her dinner table, the guy who'd shot himself in the foot
in a rubber boat in the middle of a state park lake on Memorial Day
would be revealed to have been not only drunk but also
recently promoted in the sheriff's department and subject
to wife with a small dog bred by someone they both knew in high-school.
The dog bites.

This is something she does—burrow into the facts,
cut tunnels between them,
aerate—it's a habit of knowing she'd acquired by being raised
in a funeral home, the family's trade one of safe predictions.

The soil she'd knocked off the roots stains the sidewalk.
Pretty soon, she'll have to find someone to take some of her bulbs.

2007, Richmond, VA

III

She has written today. He can picture her looking out her window,
the sunken living room a soft bowl behind her back. She told him
she watched the city marathon runners cross the width of her drive-way.
So many traveled at awkward, misshapen gaits. She saw a man wearing a tutu
and the patent ridiculousness of it was enough
to make her cry because she knew she could never impose
herself on the world with such impunity.

He could see her the way she saw that runner,
her view bisected by the mature poplar, its dangling
flowers. He knew how many of them, shed by exigencies
of sexual reproduction, fall each day
onto her front steps. He used to sweep them up for her
when he came to do the yard work, and wished
he could do so again.

2012, Washington, D.C., Arts of War

IV

On the bus, he is thinking of god.
The seat is hard, it is of a piece with the whole metal shell
that vibrates over the Memorial Bridge cobblestone,
left there to slow the traffic.

The bus is going east. It is early, but it is also March, and he can look
at the sun through the mass of air, solid and speckled
above the river like a block of ice unpacked from a straw-filled crate:
the sun is a large round thing, quite available.

Sun Tzu would say, dig the wells,
knock the wheels off your wagons,
build a stockade—
in all ways obscure your urge to retreat.

He laughs at the mind's ability to offer up Sun Tzu
when the rest of him has been swept free of thought.
The doors of perception are cleansed
by abject fear and stand wide open. This gaping void
he intuits to be a proper place for god,

a trap, in fact. Consider the bait:
he has surrendered his soul, quite freely—
it had become, somehow, less than human, it had been
terrorized like an occupied city, and the last
human thing in it was this ability to watch
and wonder if this is how it really works.

At the end of the bridge, the bus turns left.
He sees traces of gilding on the feathered hoofs
of the winged war horse.

2012, Washington, D.C., Arts of Peace

V

The hour he can never recall is the one
in which he began to believe what he was being told,
the prognosis far from the worst,
the pain a shipwreck, a survivor of something
that was no longer there.
No omen, but a ghost.

He remembers it was shortly after four when he left the building,
an afternoon in April, a storm rolling up the Potomac. Outside,
four uniformed Marines had lowered the flag. He saw their hands,
sharp in the umber light, beating down on the stripes,
the silk alive, bucking them off, the billows of it
high above their heads. The yokes banged and snapped.
The wind thumbed his chest.
He felt the work of being afraid done.

At the traffic light, lilacs whipped in the wind, and the smell
slapped on the sidewalk heavy as wet laundry.

The homeless man on the other side watched him cross,
looked him in the eye over his mirrored sunglasses,
said, Fuck you,
what are you lookin' at?

2014, Vilnius, Lithuania

VI

I met the Colonel once. Through the window
the snow on the tall chestnuts in the park
appeared blue, as if already more in touch with water
than with itself.

I remember he had a very small notebook
and was wearing a tie in hunter green
with tiny shapes of copper-skinned pointers
facing east and west. I had never known him
to have an actual dog, but I'd like to think he wanted one,
dreamt of one, in fact, in that responsible way
that fully grants all the reasons why the dream's attainment
is impossible but proceeds anyway.

The talk was of drones, and I wanted to leave,
but couldn't, so I studied the man's hands,
small, square and serene. Later, someone told me he'd flown
things. It was easy to picture—the even contact
his fingers would have made with the grips,
his attention. From certain altitudes
things on the ground look remarkably recognizable—
yet distant—the repertoire of human ingenuity
ultimately limited. He'd have seen things
with square roofs, things with domed roofs,
things without roofs, perhaps, and those
that is roofs for what is below.

Minimize considered

I let the day slip unguarded
I clean shoes preparing
for the time we can go out walking
I buy coffee
discuss the scarce repertoire
of our diversions
conclude
we are indeed in want
of a crossword puzzle compendium

outside
a rooftop crane has begun
to redraw the things we see
it turns
bisects the view into triangles

I can hear voices in the hallway
new tenants no doubt
to replace the neighbors whose names
we never learned

at night
we listen for the sounds
of the small animal that we think lives
above us
usually we can hear him chase a toy
the scatter of his nails on hardwood floors
sometimes he slips

June

a circus of rain

drops spring-loaded like acrobatic fleas
grass—in tufts
dogs—in streaky fur
the lindens—as lush as they must be
to contribute to this Arcadian endeavor:
Washington, D. C.

The pavement—dappled mirror—
returns my gaze as winks.

June, Hoary Plantain
> *A common plant along footpaths, it was considered to be one of the nine sacred herbs by the ancient Saxon people.*

seed heads ensconced in lilac inflorescence
each wand sways gently on an arched pale stem
minute tethered zeppelins
they foment their own
benign and secret ends

aloof
        they spring aloft behind my grazing hand

All enemies, foreign and domestic
> *Residents report sighting coyotes in New York City's outer boroughs*

the first one appeared in the *Times* on a Wednesday in April
a reedy coagulation of wildness in the receding darkness of the Brooklyn
    Park
a female
the first sighted in seventy years
a strain on credulity
a ghost

a pair is certain now to inhabit Staten Island
I picture them: grainy warm concrete
under their compact paws as they surveyed the angular expanse
of suburbia from the elevation of an unnamed off ramp
like John Smith fresh alit on the shores of Chesapeake Bay
teaching himself the new horizon

a preposterous fiction of course

the terrain must have unspooled before them
triggered affirmative something in the pleats of their old DNA
canis latrans remembering its way home

the dogs in their initial placidity can be forgiven
citizens of a liberal democracy they were
outright bourgeois on their lawns
ensconced objects of our pieties—
rule of law
sanctity of the home

can the coyotes really be said to steal
when the fences they cross are invisible—
to all but the unfortunate dogs

the poodle must now transcend his haircut
the pit bull must part with his pillow
and I must look for a metaphor less perfect than this:
fifteen years in this country but still
some days I am the coyote and some days
I am the dog

Cooking Dinner on the Night before Moving

the luggage expectant
for days
      aimless as a vacant cab
cruising

a splitting off
bonds cracked
      gravitational fields disrupted
your things—wedged off my orbit—
depart

our glass-eyed nucleus—this space—
keeps spinning
aloft the concrete sidewalks
pale as ice

no heat unleashed
no light
an onion peeled
your hand absorbs
the grudging scud of knife

Nina Murray holds degrees in linguistics and creative writing. She has translated Oksana Zabuzhko's *The Museum of Abandoned Secrets* as well as *Fish* and *Stargorod* by Peter Aleshkovsky. Her original poetry has appeared in *Lumina, Cosmonauts' Avenue, Canthius, Ekphrasis,* and other journals. Three poems were included in *The Untidy Season*, an anthology of work by Nebraska women poets. She is a career member of the U.S. Foreign Service. This is her first book.

www.ingramcontent.com/pod-product-compliance
Lightning Source LLC
LaVergne TN
LVHW041507070426
835507LV00012B/1390